T0021096

THE CHILDREN'S BOOK OF
BIRDWATCHING

THE CHILDREN'S BOOK OF
BIRDWATCHING

Written by Dan Rouse

Contents

Introduction

Birds are all around us. You might not always notice them, but they're there. Nesting in trees, clattering on rooftops, bathing in puddles, and hopping along on the ground. If you start paying more attention to birds, you'll discover that they are endlessly fascinating. Different types of birds have different features, habits, and skills—and you can learn about these just by watching them.

You can help birds, too. They need safe places to nest, breed, eat, and drink. There are lots of simple ways to be kind to birds, by offering them what they need. And by helping birds, you help other wildlife—and the planet as well! So, look around. What birds do you see? Are you ready to learn more about them? Come on, let's go!

Let's go birdwatching!

Birds are fascinating! If you take a moment to sit and watch for birds, you'll see how they move and flutter, you'll notice their various colors, and you'll hear their beautiful birdsong.

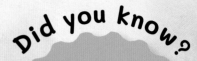
Why are birds important?

Plants and wildlife would not thrive without birds. Birds eat aphids, caterpillars, snails, and slugs, which stops these creatures from eating plants. Birds also help spread seeds from trees and other plants.

You can hang some bird feeders to offer birds a safe place to rest and find food.

Know your birds

Do you know how to name the parts of a bird's body? Knowing how to spot the difference between the same features on different birds will help you identify the birds you see.

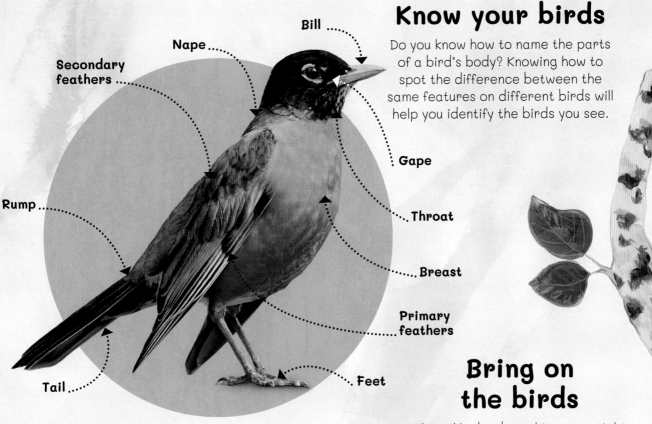

- Bill
- Nape
- Secondary feathers
- Rump
- Tail
- Gape
- Throat
- Breast
- Primary feathers
- Feet

Bring on the birds

If you like birdwatching, you might want to find out how to attract birds to your local outdoor space, whether that's your backyard, balcony, or park!

Bird benefits

Bringing birds to your outdoor space benefits you! Birds eat insects that might eat your plants, their song can help you relax and enjoy nature—and they bring many more benefits as well!

Eastern Screech-Owls eat rodents and insects that feed on plants.

Northern Mockingbirds have their own song and mimic other birds.

Where to find birds

Birds feed and nest in all sorts of places, so having an outdoor space with lots of options will give you the best chance of attracting many kinds of birds. Here are some of the most common places to spot birds around you.

In the treetops
You might spot fast-flying warblers zooming among the treetops, where they are less of a target for predators.

On trees
Many birds, including Blue Jays, perch up high to get the best view. Some birds, such as Brown Creepers, are camouflaged in trees.

Inside trees
Holes in tree trunks provide shelter. Flycatchers nest in large holes, while woodpeckers prefer to peck out deeper nesting holes.

Flowers
Flowers attract insects, and insects attract many birds!

On the ground
Larger birds, such as thrushes, spend lots of time on the ground searching for food. Smaller birds, including wrens and sparrows, hop among shrubs and bushes.

Did you know?

Being able to feed safely away from predators is the most important thing for birds.

Yellow Warbler

American Robin

Bushes provide protection from predators.

Foliage is denser in spring and summer.

A high perch offers birds the best view for spotting food and predators.

Blue Jay

Think about it!

Does your outdoor space have any features birds will like? Can you think of anything you could do to make it a better space for birds?

Red-bellied Woodpecker

Top tip

Having a mix of trees, shrubs, plants, and ground space will help create the perfect environment for birds.

Garden birds

Some birds live, feed, and breed in the same small area their whole lives, which might be your backyard or a nearby green space. Others are only around for part of the year. Watching them helps you learn their individual habits. Here are some common birds.

American Robin

With their red breasts, robins are easy to pick out. They are very territorial, which means they fiercely protect their feeding and breeding areas from other birds. Robins are often seen hopping around lawns, stopping sometimes to pull an earthworm from the ground.

House Wren

These birds love living near people, in cities and on farms. Every gardener's helper, they hunt insects that would otherwise eat plants. In addition to nesting in nest boxes, they also find other hollow spaces for nests—such as mailboxes and old boots.

Tufted Titmouse

These birds whistle a "peter, peter, peter" song nearly year-round. They often use hair plucked from animals to line their nests and will take seeds from feeding trays to crack open away from other birds.

Baltimore Oriole

The male Baltimore Oriole has brilliant orange and black feathers, while the female is yellow-orange and gray. Once the leaves come out on the trees, these birds can be heard more often than seen while they forage for insects high in the treetops. They sing a unique whistling song.

Draw it!

Pick a bird that you like the look of. Can you draw or paint it? Think about the shape of its bill, its coloring, and what its feathers look like.

Northern Mockingbird

The mockingbird's beautiful voice and song meant that it used to be popular as a house pet. Thankfully, capturing mockingbirds has now been outlawed, and this bird can sing freely.

American Goldfinch

These bright birds often arrive in a noisy flock, called a charm. Other finches, such as Pine Siskins, often flock with them. American Goldfinches are especially drawn to feeders with niger seeds.

Did you know?

American Goldfinches molt in the winter, regrowing feathers in the spring. Only males are bright yellow.

House Finch

These birds are another regular backyard visitor, often seen together in groups. They are quite vocal and may be heard singing from a high perch at any time of the year. Male House Finches look similar to Purple Finches—but their feathers are a brighter red.

Chipping Sparrow

The Chipping Sparrow is a small bird with a bright rusty cap, found in yards across the country. During the summer, you're likely to hear the male's distinctive, long, buzzy trill in the branches of a nearby tree.

Research it!

Which of your regular feathered visitors do you like best? Choose a bird that you've seen near your home and try to find out more about it. Research everything you can think of:

- What it looks like
- Bill shape
- Diet
- Birdsong
- Habits
- Likes and dislikes
- What else can you think of?

With a little research, you can become an expert!

The seasons

Some birds migrate. They fly from one area to another to find food to eat in each season and to travel from their home base to breeding sites. Look for the arrival of migrating birds at different times of the year.

Barn Swallow

Wintering in South America, Barn Swallow begin their journey north in February, spreading out over much of North Americ by May. They feed on insects, before creating cuplike nests.

Purple Martin

This bird travels to the Midwestern and Eastern states of the US from the Amazon basin. It nests in the eaves of houses and holes in trees in small groups.

Spring and summer

Migrating visitors often return to the same area—and even the same nest—year after year. They will spend the spring and summer months building nests, breeding, feeding, and raising the next generation.

Scarlet Tanager

These birds breed in eastern North America and winter in South America. They migrate at night and arrive in the US in bursts, depending on how far they have traveled.

Fall and winter

Migrating birds fly south from colder climates to escape the harsh weather and live where food is more easily available. They settle in noisy flocks and huddle together at night to keep warm.

American Tree Sparrow

These tiny birds breed in the northernmost part of North America before making their way down to the center of the continent. They migrate in flocks during the night.

Bohemian Waxwing

These colorful birds form large flocks that roam south from their breeding grounds across the northern US and Canada. They are attracted to fruit trees.

White-throated Sparrow

These birds return from their breeding grounds in the colder climates of Canada and Alaska to the southern parts of the US. They are found at the edges of woods or backyards.

Bird spotting

As you learn more about the birds around you, you will soon be able to recognize some of them. Look for their noticeable features. What color are their feathers? What shape is their tail?

Bands

Blue Jays have black bands on their blue tail feathers.

Feathers

The colors and patterns of bird feathers vary widely. They can give you important clues as to which bird you are looking for.

Patterns

Barn Owls have a striped pattern on their wings.

Shimmering

Ruby-throated Hummingbirds have shimmering green feathers on their backs.

Rose-breasted Grosbeaks have a red triangle on their breasts.

Shapes

Feather type

A bird has a variety of feather types on its body, and these feathers look different, depending on the species. Even the tiniest feather contains so many clues!

Flight feathers

These strong, wide feathers provide lift while flying. The shaft runs through one side.

Body feathers

These have a soft, fluffy base and a smooth top.

Tail shape

When you see birds flying overhead, their tail shape is one of the first things you'll notice.

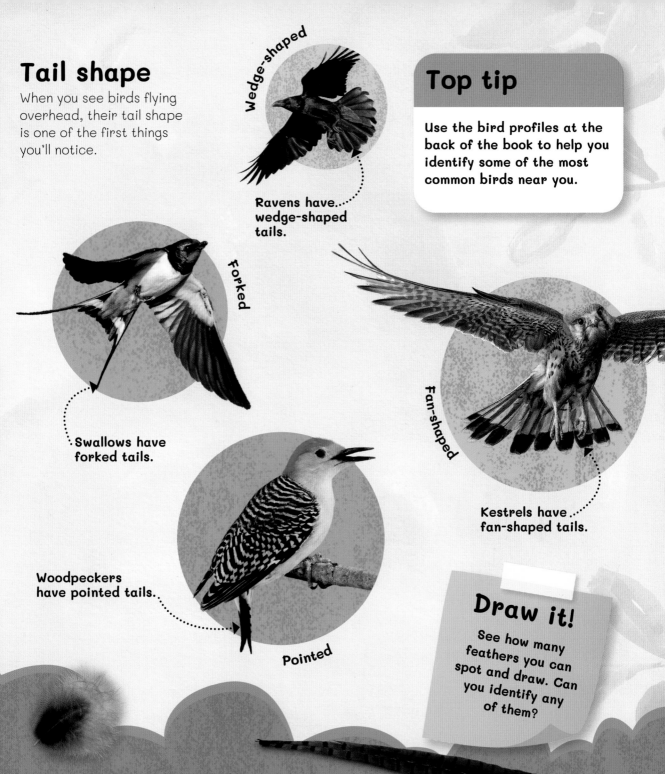

Wedge-shaped

Ravens have wedge-shaped tails.

Top tip

Use the bird profiles at the back of the book to help you identify some of the most common birds near you.

Forked

Swallows have forked tails.

Fan-shaped

Kestrels have fan-shaped tails.

Woodpeckers have pointed tails.

Pointed

Draw it!

See how many feathers you can spot and draw. Can you identify any of them?

Downy feathers

These soft, fluffy feathers keep the bird warm.

Tail feathers

Long, strong tail feathers help birds balance. The shaft runs down the middle.

What birds need

If you want to attract birds, you should focus on the four things birds need the most—food, water, plants, and a place to nest. A combination of these things will attract birds to your outdoor space all year round.

Food

Birds prefer to eat different things—some like insects from a pond, while others prefer berries from a bush. Some species will also eat from a bird feeder or pond that you've set up outside your home.

Water

Birds will drink from any water, whether it's a natural pool or a little birdbath— just as long as it is safe from predators. Water is also a habitat for the prey of some birds, such as insects and frogs.

Northern Mockingbird

Look for Northern Mockingbirds in berry bushes any time of the year.

Plants

Every outdoor space, from balconies to backyards, can be a home to plants. Plants are good for birds in many ways: they attract insects, grow berries and flowers, and offer shelter. Their leaves also collect dew and rainwater for birds to drink.

A place to nest

There are lots of ways you can offer nesting places for your feathered friends. Think about where might be a good spot around your home—from your house's outer walls and eaves to trees, plants, and fences.

FOOD

The simplest way to attract and feed birds is by putting up a bird feeder. If you learn about the types of food and feeders available, you can create a space that will appeal to all kinds of birds. Once birds discover the food is there (often surprisingly quickly), they will keep coming back for more!

On trees

Trees are an essential source of seeds, fruits, insects, and larvae for birds to feed on. Even seed-eaters need caterpillars for their chicks.

Finding food

A bird's size and diet, and even the type of feet and bill it has, make a huge difference in where it will look for food. Your outdoor space may be full of places where birds might search for meals.

Woodpeckers use their long, slender beaks to search cracks in bark for insects.

On the ground

Larger birds and foragers eat insects and worms from the ground. They will also happily feast on any food that has spilled from a bird feeder.

Robins mostly feed on the ground, looking for invertebrates, such as worms.

In trees

Some birds collect nuts and larger pieces of food and store them inside holes in trees, especially during colder months. These hoarders are very protective of their stashes!

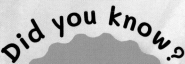

Birds eat little and often, so they prefer nutritious foods that give them bursts of energy.

Chickadees hide seeds and nuts in tree crevices to eat later.

In shrubs

Flowers and shrubs are perfect places for a bit of foraging. Some birds rely on the protection shrubs offer so they can feed without being afraid of predators.

Wrens feed in shrubs and flower beds to avoid predators.

Observe it!

Make a scrapbook about the birds you see near your home. Take photos, print them out, and add dates and other details. Do you spot the same birds all the time?

What do birds eat?

Garden birds mainly eat seeds, nuts, fruit, berries, caterpillars, worms, and insects. You can buy some of these foods, and human-made bird food, to put out in your garden or yard. Birds of prey might also swoop down to hunt rodents, such as mice.

Suet cake

This block of fat is filled with other food, such as seeds. It is a great source of nutrients and fat for adult and young birds. Many birds love suet cakes, but particularly woodpeckers.

Did you know?

Suet cake comes in some very interesting flavors, from berry to insect!

Peanuts

High in energy, unsalted peanuts are a favorite for most birds. Larger birds can use their strong bills to crack open unshelled peanuts, but shelled nuts are better for smaller birds, such as chickadees.

Sunflower seeds

Nutritious sunflower seeds are especially useful in winter, when it's harder to find food. Jays, finches, chickadees, siskins, titmice, cardinals, grosbeaks, and juncos alll love these seeds.

During breeding season, soak dried mealworms in water so young birds can digest them easily.

Mealworms

Dried mealworms are perfect for insect-eaters, such as starlings. They are a good source of fat and protein, and can be added to seed mixes or simply spread on a tray.

Safflower seeds

Safflower seeds are high in protein, fat, and fiber—all of which birds need to stay healthy. Jays, finches, doves, and many other birds love these small seeds.

Make it yourself

You can buy these items from your local pet store, but you can also make your own. Turn the page to learn how.

You will need:

Bowl Seeds **Nuts and dried fruit** **Vegetable shortening**

DIY bird food

Bird food is easy and fun to make. Suet balls contain seeds, nuts, and dried fruits mixed with suet (which is usually meat fat, but vegetable shortening works, too). These suet balls are delicious and nutritious!

1. Add your seeds and suet
Pour the seeds you want to use into a bowl. Add little chunks of vegetable shortening.

2. Mix together
Use the warmth of your hands to soften the shortening and mix the seeds in until you have a soft, sticky mixture.

3. Form into shapes

Mold the mixture into the shape you want. You can make balls, cubes, or even stars! Smooth the edges so they hold together.

4. Leave to set

Place the shapes in an open container in the fridge to firm up. Once they are set, put them into your bird feeders.

Seed mix

Use the ingredients below to make your own mix. Adapt for different birds.

Quantities

Aim for:

- 2 cups filler (to give texture)
- 1 cup bulk (main nutrition)
- ½ cup fat (for extra energy)

Filler ideas:

Oats, crushed eggshells, cooked rice, cereal, fruit and vegetable seeds, crumbled pastry

Bulk ideas:

Sunflower seeds, chopped unsalted nuts, cereal, bread crumbs, cooked diced potato, raisins and dried fruit, diced fruit peel

Fat ideas:

Unsalted butter, grated cheese, shortening, unsalted suet

Bird feeders

There are all sorts of bird feeders, and each one has been designed with different birds and food in mind. When choosing a feeder, think about the types of bird you want to attract and what foods are best for them.

Bird food comes in cakes, balls, and pellets.

Suet feeder

These have a large mesh for easy access to the food without the danger of birds getting stuck.

Suitable for: Woodpeckers, sparrows, and long-clawed birds

Table feeder

You can adapt these for any type of food and any outdoor space.

Suitable for: All types of bird, depending on the size of the table

Table feeders come in all shapes and sizes.

Food is off the ground so it won't sprout.

Ground feeder

These are easy to clean. Change the food to attract different birds.

Suitable for: All types of bird, especially larger birds

Mesh feeder

These are best for larger food items, such as peanuts and suet pellets. They are not ideal for seed mixes.

Suitable for: Birds with long claws, such as tits, nuthatches, and woodpeckers

Birds will grasp the bars and hang on to the feeder to eat.

Go for a feeder with more holes to attract flocks of birds.

Tube feeder

You can hang these anywhere and use them for most seed mixes.

Suitable for: Finches and birds with long claws and short beaks

Some wall feeders come with suckers to attach to windows.

Top tip

Set up more than one type of feeder to create a whole feeding station!

Wall feeder

Attach these to walls, fences, or windows. They hold any seed mix.

Suitable for: Some finches and long-clawed, short-billed birds, such as robins and jays

Whose bill is best?

Birds have many different bill shapes, and this affects what kinds of food they can eat. If you want to offer food to birds, you need to think about what food different birds eat—and where they can find it!

Evening Grosbill

The seed crusher

Finches have superstrong bills for crushing seeds. Larger bills can crush big seeds, while others are fine enough to pick up soft seeds from a flower.

Swainson's Thrush

Northern Flicker

The ground pecker

Foraging birds have longer bills for digging down into the ground to search for worms. Long bills are also perfect for eating from a bird feeder, or even digging into an apple!

The drummer

Woodpecker bills are strong, thick, and sturdy. They are ideal for pecking or digging for insects, and for reaching into feeders for nuts.

American Kestrel

The meat-eater

Birds that eat animals are called birds of prey. They have short, sharp, strong bills for tearing into food. They catch prey on the ground or in the air and then find a perch on which to eat it.

White-throated Sparrow

The picker-upper

Small, ground-dwelling birds have short bills and eat easy-to-find food, such as flies, seeds, and berries. They love food that is easy to pick up, such as seeds from a feeding table.

Feeding birds in your yard

Bird feeders are great for some birds. But what about species that like to hunt or forage for themselves, such as thrushes or kestrels? For those birds, you need to attract insects, too.

Flat feeders, such as this one, are perfect for finches and sparrows, which love to feed on seeds.

Ivy attracts insects, which means thrushes and other foragers will come along for a snack!

You will need:

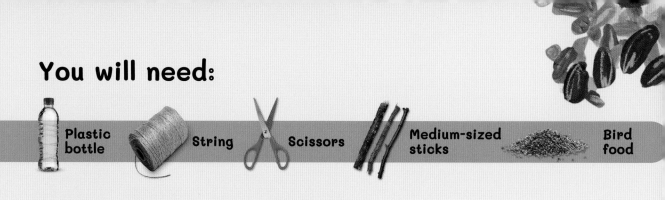

Plastic bottle   **String**   **Scissors**   **Medium-sized sticks**   **Bird food**

DIY bird feeder

A bird feeder is a great way to attract birds and offer them the food they need. Instead of buying a bird feeder, why not use an old plastic bottle and make one yourself?

Ask an adult to help!

1. Prepare the bottle

Clean out the bottle and decorate it if you like. Then, tie a piece of string or twine just under the lid so it's ready to be hung later.

2. Make holes

Ask an adult to use scissors or a screwdriver to poke two holes towards the base of the bottle, opposite each other, and two larger feeding holes higher up.

3. Make perches

Next, you need to add perches—something for birds to hold on to while they feed. Thread your sticks into the smaller holes you made. Now you have perfect perches!

4. Fill with bird food

Pour your seed mix into the bottle. You may want to use a funnel to avoid any mess.

Birds to watch for

Different birds use different feeders. This bottle feeder will attract species with long claws that can grasp the sticks.

5. Hang it up!

Where is a good place to hang your feeder? Think of quiet spots away from people—and cats! Birds like a nearby place to perch while they wait their turn to eat.

Nuthatch

These fiery birds can expertly hold onto branches with their long claws. This helps them reach food, such as insects.

Evening Grosbeak

These birds loves sunflower seeds. You might spot them at your feeder in winter if you live in the northern US or Canada.

NESTS

Birds make nests in safe places, away from predators. Here, they can lay eggs and raise their young. You can help your local birds by setting up nest boxes in ideal spots. If birds nest in your outdoor space, you may be able to observe their behavior—such as how they feed their young.

Spot the nest!

Nests are not homes for birds, but seasonal places where they can lay eggs and raise chicks. Birds choose their nesting spots carefully. Some nest high up in trees, while others nest near ground level.

 High up
The higher the nest, the safer it is from ground predators—but it is more vulnerable to attacks from above.

 In the open
To avoid ground predators, pigeons and doves nest high up in trees, shrubs, and hedges so they can see any predators approaching.

3 Holes
Holes in tree trunks offer great protection, so many birds nest in them, including woodpeckers, owls, and nuthatches.

 Shrubs
Thrushes typically nest in shrubs or hedges, where they have some protection. Brown Thrashers create cup-shaped nests in shrubs.

Did you know?

Finches build nests on branches, using twigs and moss. The twigs are often stuck together with spider silk.

Mourning Doves make messy, loose nests of twigs that rest on branches.

2 Mourning Dove

Blackbirds use twigs, moss, and leaves to weave bowl-shaped nests lined with grass.

 Red-winged Blackbird

1 Black-billed Magpie

Unlike jays and crows, magpies nest in groups.

3 Eastern Screech-Owl

These owls build their nests in large holes in old trees.

Spot it!

Owls and woodpeckers choose deep tree holes, while starlings choose holes with small entrances to keep predators out. The next time you go for a walk, see if you can spot any tree holes.

Nest boxes

Nest boxes provide shelter for adult and baby birds. They give birds a safe place to lay eggs and raise their young. Which type of nest box can you spot around you?

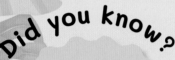

Many gardens and green spaces have too few plants and trees, or are being paved over. Nest boxes are a safe place for birds who can't find a nest spot.

Standard box

 These have wooden walls, a small entrance hole, and a sloping roof to keep the rain out.

Ideal for: Eastern Bluebirds and House Sparrows

Location: 5—6½ ft (1½—2 m) off the ground

Swallow nesting cup

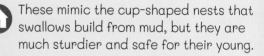 These mimic the cup-shaped nests that swallows build from mud, but they are much sturdier and safe for their young.

Ideal for: Swallows

Location: Inside outbuildings or garages (as long as the door is always open), or under the eaves of roofs

Open-fronted box

 The open front and deep base allow a nesting bird to sit securely with a good view of its surroundings.

 Ideal for: American Robins and Mourning Doves

Location: Among ivy on walls, fences, or trees

Top tip

Smaller birds, such as sparrows, use nest boxes with smaller holes. Larger birds, such as House Sparrows, look for larger-holed boxes.

Purple Martin box

Purple Martins nest close to one another, so this box has lots of spaces for nests.

 Ideal for: Purple Martins

Location: Out in the semi-open air

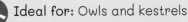

Raptor box

Birds of prey like trees near open land, so raptor boxes can be found in outdoor spaces that offer these conditions.

Ideal for: Owls and kestrels

Location: $11\frac{1}{2}$–16 ft ($3\frac{1}{2}$–5 m) off the ground. Under cover of trees for owls; with open access near a field for kestrels

Teardrop nesting pocket

🏠 These are perfect for birds that roost or nest in deeper spaces.

🐦 **Ideal for:** Wrens and chickadees

📍 **Location:** Just inside the leaves of shrubs or trees

Woodpecker box

🏠 These are similar to a standard nest box, but deep enough for woodpeckers to look after their eggs and raise their chicks.

🐦 **Ideal for:** Woodpeckers

📍 **Location:** On tree trunks, 10—16 ft (3—5 m) off the ground

Creeper box

🏠 Brown Creepers like tree holes. They use their claws to grip the bark as they go in. Creeper boxes offer similar conditions.

🐦 **Ideal for:** Brown Treecreepers

📍 **Location:** On tree trunks

Canopy

For birds that want an open nest, these nesting pockets offer extra stability, and a roof for shelter.

Ideal for: Thrushes and doves

Location: Among the leaves of shrubs or tied to a shrub's branches

Side pocket

For birds that like an easy exit, these nests have large entrance holes.

Ideal for: Nuthatches and wrens

Location: Settled in trees or inside outbuildings or open-door sheds

Look around!

Can you see any nests? Keep a photo diary by taking a photo of the nest every week. See if you can spot any changes over time.

Unexpected nests

Birds are naturally curious and inventive. They sometimes choose surprising places to nest. You can help birds out by offering them nesting places made from everyday items. What unusual objects will you use?

Teapots

All sorts of kitchen items can be used to offer birds a home, from old bowls to teapots. A teapot will certainly be a curious addition to your nest box collection!

Old boots

Just about any kind of worn-out boot can be turned into a nesting spot. Secure a walking boot so the hole is facing forward as an entrance.

Place the boot toe-down to reduce the amount of water that can enter.

Hang the teapot by the handle on a hedge or tree. The spout makes a good drainage hole.

Place the crate in a sheltered corner or behind potted shrubs.

Hang baskets on an evergreen tree, if possible, to keep leaves from falling into the basket in fall.

Plastic crates

Plastic crates are ideal for birds that like to nest in colonies or on a nesting "shelf." Place the crate on its side and add straw, moss, or twigs to attract birds inside.

Hanging baskets

These are perfect for birds that like open nests. You can buy hanging baskets or use a household item like a colander. Line it with moss, twigs, and feathers, and hang it up!

Gather it!

If you don't have old items to turn into a nest right now, use natural materials. Gather twigs, straw, and moss—and get creative!

Nest box spots

Where you put your nest box is very important. It needs to be somewhere birds can access easily, a safe place—of course—and a place where they want to nest!

 Tree
Most nest boxes can be placed in trees. Make sure there is open space around the box entrance so birds can fly in and out easily.

 Fence
A fence is a good place for small, open-fronted nest boxes. Pick a spot where there aren't too many plants by the fence, which is where predators can hide.

 Under the roof
This is the best spot for swallow nest boxes, because the roof provides much-needed shelter.

4 Wall
Try to keep your nest box 5 ft (1.5 m) above the ground, so it's away from predators.

3

!

Ask an adult to attach the nest box if it needs to go high-up—or if it needs screws or nails to attach it.

4

Top tips

⌗ Think about which way the nest box faces. If it is a sunny spot, the birds might overheat.

⌗ Tilt the box slightly forward so rainwater drips out. You don't want your box to get flooded!

⌗ Avoid places near flat ledges, where predators can perch.

⌗ Regularly check that any wall fixings are secure.

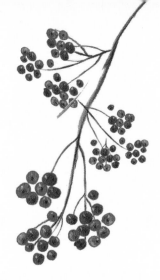

PLANTS

If chosen well, plants can provide shelter and a source of food for birds—both of which are very important! If you add bird-friendly plants to your outdoor space, you will be offering leaves, flowers, nesting materials, and food, so that birds can find what they need all year round.

What's so great about plants?

Plants offer many natural benefits and are a great way to help your local birds. Birds will visit any green space, but you can make your yard or balcony more appealing by thinking carefully about the plants you choose.

Soil

Healthy soil is key for healthy plants. Soil affects all the creatures birds feed on, so use organic compost.

Flowers

Nectar-rich flowers attract insects, which birds will come to feast on. Some birds even feed directly on plants such as snapdragons.

Leaves

All sorts of leafy plants and vegetables attract butterflies. Their caterpillars are a favorite food source for birds.

Fruit and berries

Fruit trees and berry shrubs are vital sources of energy in winter. They also offer leaves for birds to hide in and roost.

Wild corners

Make space for wild plants, such as weeds, grasses, and wildflowers. Their seed heads are very popular with birds!

Did you know?

Birds are part of the ecosystem. If all parts of the system are working well, the wildlife will flourish!

House Sparrow

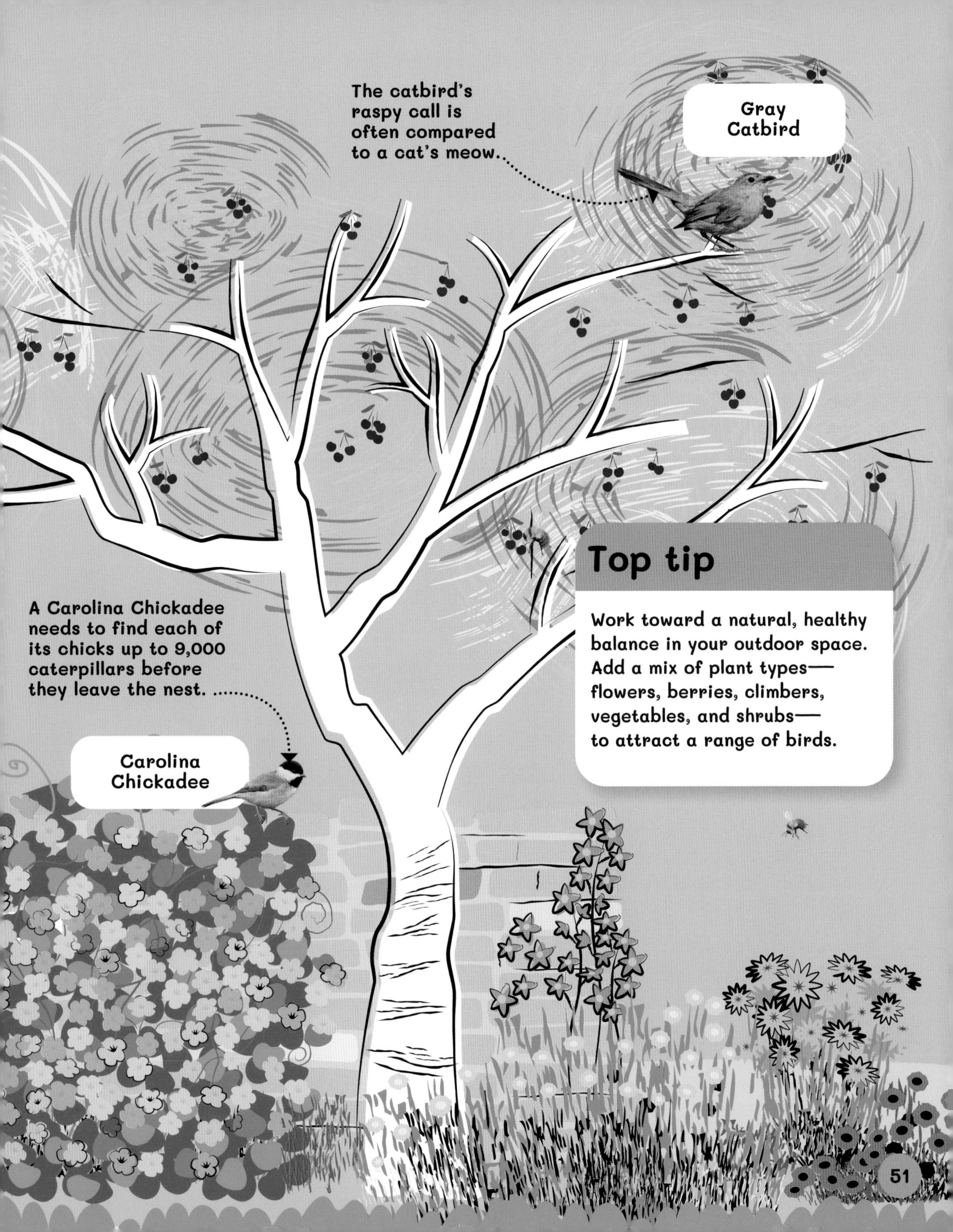

The catbird's raspy call is often compared to a cat's meow.

Gray Catbird

A Carolina Chickadee needs to find each of its chicks up to 9,000 caterpillars before they leave the nest.

Carolina Chickadee

Top tip

Work toward a natural, healthy balance in your outdoor space. Add a mix of plant types—flowers, berries, climbers, vegetables, and shrubs—to attract a range of birds.

Perfect plants

Plants support birds and other wildlife throughout the year, providing nesting materials, shelter, and food. Different plants offer different benefits to birds.

Shrubs for shelter

Shrubs make an ideal safe space for birds. Evergreen shrubs offer shelter all year round, while deciduous shrubs flower or grow berries in warmer months, attracting birds and insects.

Lavender
In addition to its lovely smell, lavender attracts insects and is easy to grow in both sunny and shady spots.

Camellia
This evergreen shrub has large leaves that offer shelter. Its vivid pink blooms attract insects, which birds will come to dine on!

Spotted laurel
This dense, evergreen shrub grows best in the shade and is great for nesting birds.

Elder
Elder grows best in cooler climates. In the fall, the elderberries are a popular snack for visiting birds.

Kousa dogwood
This tree produces fruit toward the end of summer and into the fall. Its knobby red fruit is enjoyed by many garden birds, such as Northern Mockingbirds.

Top tip

Layer your plants to create a varied habitat for birds— and to make the most of your outdoor space.

Nectar-rich flowers

Flowering plants provide nectar for insects, such as bees, moths, butterflies, and hoverflies. A mix of day- and night-flowering plants will attract insects—and the birds who love to eat them!

Buddleja

This heavily scented plant has large purple flowers that are best for attracting butterflies.

Woods' rose

The open flowers of this climbing plant make it easy for butterflies to perch and feed. Birds will be quick to follow.

Foxglove

This pretty plant is easy to grow. Its tall, richly scented flowers will attract so many insects, birds will come flocking!

Evening primrose

At night, the open, yellow flowers bloom. They often attract hawkmoths, which are a tasty treat for birds!

Honeysuckle is a great option for small outdoor spaces, as it can grow up a trellis or fence.

Night gladiolus

This plant blooms at night. The tunnel-like flowers attract all sorts of smaller moth species.

Garden phlox

Ideal for planting in small containers, the bright, open flowers attract hummingbirds and moths for birds to feast on.

Honeysuckle

The sweet-smelling flowers of this climbing plant attract plenty of bees during the summer.

Cherry

Soft, sweet cherries ripen in the summer and are popular with thrushes.

Thrushes might thank you for the cherries with their lovely song!

Raspberry

Juicy raspberries grow throughout summer and fall. They are a firm favorite of warblers, chickadees, and wrens.

Crab apple

In the fall and winter, small apples grow, attracting American Robins and some thrushes. The birds may compete for the apples!

Mountain ash

The bright red berries really stand out in the winter. They are loved by waxwings, thrushes, and starlings.

Viburnum

In the fall, bright berries bloom on this leafy shrub. They attract bullfinches and mistle thrushes.

Fruits and berries for food

Fruit trees and bushes provide food for both birds and humans. If you plan your plants well, you can offer food for birds throughout the year.

Blackberry

They might be thorny, but blackberry bushes provide shelter and large, juicy berries throughout the summer.

Holly

The dense, evergreen holly leaves offer valuable winter shelter, while the bright berries are a tasty treat for birds!

54

Seeds for food

Seeded flowers provide food for birds, and the seeds can be harvested, too. You can make bird food with the seeds, or just grow flowers to help local wildlife thrive!

Millet

Millet and sorghum seeds are simple to harvest and great for bird feeders.

Sweat pea

Sweet pea is easy to plant in containers or pots, and it attracts many birds.

Thistle

The fine seeds are good for seed mixes, especially popular with finches.

Dahlia

Dahlia seed heads are a good source of food after the flowers have faded.

Foxglove

The nectar-rich flowers attract insects and nectar-feeding birds, such as warblers. The seeds are easy to harvest and resow.

Cornflower

These flowers attract insects. Then, once the flowers have gone, the seed heads are a good source of food for birds.

Sunflower

The large seeds are ideal for seed mixes and perfect to leave out for birds to feed on naturally.

Plant parts

Plants provide so many things that birds need. When choosing new plants, it's not about how much space you have, but how many options you offer.

Five key elements

If you want to attract birds, you should aim to grow plants that provide these key elements:

1 Nesting material

Twigs and leaves are good examples of materials that birds use to build their nests.

2 Shelter

Leaves and foliage provide shelter for birds that will protect them from predators.

3 Insects

Bright, nectar-rich flowers attract insects, which are a popular food source for birds and their young.

4 Seeds

The seed heads of a flower are full of seeds—which are a key food for birds.

5 Fruit

Fruit or berry plants are wonderful sources of seasonal food. Birds are attracted to berries with bright colors.

Twigs

Hornbeam is a good pick because it provides lots of small twigs, as well as shelter and seeds.

Foliage

Privet, with its big leaves and dense foliage, offers a good hiding spot for many types of birds.

Flowers

Lupines and snapdragons are nectar-rich—perfect for attracting insects that birds can feed on.

Seed heads

Echinacea produce dark seed heads. If you leave them in place after the flowers have faded, birds will feed on them.

Fruit trees

Holly produces bright red berries that are easy for birds to spot, especially during the winter months.

Snapdragons grow best in a sunny spot. Plant them in your garden soil or in a container.

Think about it!

Before you add your plants, think about which parts of your outdoor space get the most sun or shade.

You will need:

Seeds   Soil   Yogurt cups

Grow your own!

It's fun to grow and harvest your own seeds. Choose a variety of plants, flowers, and vegetables for your outdoor space to invite a diverse range of birds!

1. Getting started

Buy seeds or harvest some from wildflowers. You can also try a local seed swap to find plants that thrive naturally in your area.

2. Sowing

Sow your seeds in weed-free soil—directly into the ground or in small containers that you will transfer later. Water them regularly.

3. Flowering

Enjoy the beautiful blooms when your plants flower. Watch as their nectar and bright colors attract all sorts of insects and birds.

Seeds are generally ready to harvest about two months after flowering, when the flower looks dull or brown.

4. Seed heads

After flowering, your plants will turn into seed heads. Leave them be for birds to feed on or harvest the seeds to use as bird food.

5. Harvesting

Cut off the seed heads and let them dry. Then remove the seeds, using tweezers, if necessary. Store the seeds in paper envelopes.

Harvest it!

You can harvest fruit and vegetable seeds, too, such as bell pepper, melon, and tomato seeds. You can even plant tomato slices straight into your cups or soil!

6. And start again!

Use your harvested seeds. Lay them on a backyard feeder or add to a seed mix. Or sow them and grow another generation of plants!

Top tip

Plants that grow and flower in one year, such as sunflowers, thistle, and millet, are good to grow for seeds.

You will need:

1 cup seeds | 5 cups compost (peat-free) | Water | 2—3 cups soil

DIY seed bombs

Seed bombs are a mixture of seeds, compost, and soil that is formed into a ball. When added to soil, they scatter and grow. Seed bombs are fun to make, and they help create natural pockets of flowers for visiting wildlife to enjoy.

1. Select your seeds

Choose a mixture of seed types: small plants, stand-out feature flowers, and bushier plants.

2. Mix it up

Mix the compost into the seeds, adding a small amount of water to help them bind together.

3. Bind together

Add a little soil to the mix. This will help bind your ingredients together so they don't crumble as they dry.

4. Shape

Use your hands to form the mixture into balls and leave them in a cool, dark place to harden and dry.

5. Go wild!

Throw your seed bombs onto patches of bare soil in your yard or garden, or into prepared containers on your balcony.

Top tips

❀ The seeds of wildflowers or fruits and vegetables are good for seed bombs.

❀ Once you've thrown your seed bombs, you can either water them, so they begin to soften, or leave them to crumble and scatter into the soil naturally.

WATER

Birds need water to drink and bathe in. Ponds and water features draw in all sorts of other wildlife, too, such as insects and frogs, which birds love to eat! Adding water to your outdoor space creates a more complex ecosystem, where birds and other wildlife will thrive.

Water for birds

Birds need water to survive. It is not used just for drinking, but they also need it to keep clean. Adding water to your outdoor space introduces a whole new habitat and opens up your space to all sorts of new wildlife.

Think about it!

Think about your outdoor space. Do you have any water features? Can you think of a spot where it would be suitable to add one?

Barn Swallow

Water to drink

During hot weather, water is hard to find. In winter, puddles are iced over. So birds turn to other sources of water, such as ponds or birdbaths. Birds can drink dew or rain that collects on plants, but a clean, reliable water source is best.

Water features

There are many ways to offer water to local birds. You could build a birdbath or, if you have space, a pond. Ponds—even mini ponds—can be a place to grow water-loving plants, which, in turn, attract insects and other creatures that birds like to eat.

Black-capped Chickadee

European Starling

Water brings food

Having a water source means you are indirectly providing food for birds, too! Some birds simply love the insects and larvae that live in or near a pond, while birds of prey will be attracted by frogs and toads.

Water for bathing

Most birds use puddles and birdbaths to bathe. They splash themselves with water to remove parasites, dirt, and bacteria from their feathers.

Birdbaths

Birdbaths come in many styles, sizes, heights, and shapes. You can buy a birdbath or create your own. The best birdbath is one that suits your outdoor space. Place it where birds will feel safe and, if possible, where you can see it, too!

Raised bath

These are ideal for smaller birds, such as sparrows or robins, that like to bathe together while staying safe from predators. Raised baths also offer an easy escape route for more nervous birds, such as chickadees and wrens. Make sure the bath rests on level ground so it is stable.

Top tip

When bathing, birds can be at risk from predators, so position your birdbath somewhere birds will have a clear view in all directions. If you have a raised bath, one option is to grow thorny plants around it so animals such as cats can't get too close.

Hanging bath

These small dishes that hold water can be hung from trees or fences. They often have rough sides so birds can grip the surface and not slide off. If you hang this type of bath on a tree that sheds lots of blossoms, you might need to fish out the petals so it doesn't get too dirty.

Ground-level bath

These come in many shapes and sizes. Larger baths are good for thrushes, grackles, and doves to walk in (and they can even double as a mini pond). Make sure there is an easy way out for any non-flying animals that find their way into it—either a slope on one side or a pile of stones at the edge that will allow them to climb out.

Shallow baths up to 2 in (5 cm) deep are good for small birds with short legs. Deeper baths are ideal for larger birds, including hawks.

You will need:

 Tray   Soft soil or sand

DIY dust bath

Dust baths are perfect for small outdoor spaces. They are a great way for birds to clean bacteria and dirt from their feathers. House Sparrows, thrushes, and many other birds will happily spread their wings and wiggle around in soft soil or sand.

1. Choose your spot

Find a sunny spot for your tray on your lawn, balcony, patio, or deck—out of the way, near some plants is good.

2. Fill your tray

Add soil or sand for birds to wiggle around in. Make sure it's soft, so they don't hurt themselves!

Top tip

Use items from around your home to build your dust bath. Here are some ideas: plant tray, box, shallow bowl, plastic cookie container—or even try a trash can lid.

Observe it!

Even if you don't see any birds, check the soil or sand to see if one visited earlier. Maybe you'll notice a wing impression in the dust, where a bird has pressed its wings.

3. Build up the edges

Add stones, grass, or branches around the sides of your dust bath to help it blend in with the surroundings.

Pond life

Ponds attract amphibians, insects, and small mammals.
Some birds come to ponds to feed on these animals,
while others come to bathe and drink. Even the smallest
pond can attract more birds to your outdoor space.

Pond creatures

A pond can grow into its own
little ecosystem. Here, all
sorts of wildlife can live,
drink, breed, and shelter.

Chipmunks
may visit
ponds for
a drink.

Water boatmen
dart across
the pond's
surface.

Newts, frogs,
and toads
breed in ponds.

Top tip

Placing rocks at the
bottom of the pond
will provide good
hiding places for
some water creatures.

Ponds are good for people, too! The sound of water is calming and can help you feel relaxed.

Dragonflies and caddis flies visit ponds and lay eggs there.

Ducks might even make their way to your pond.

Why birds love ponds

Ponds offer lots of different feeding opportunities for birds. Swallows and martins may swoop down to scoop up insects from the surface of bigger ponds, while warblers and chickadees visit smaller ponds to look for food.

Helping wildlife

Different types of wildlife have different needs. With a bit of effort, you can make sure your pond is suitable for all creatures.

Have a shallow, sloping edge on one part of the pond so animals that don't live in water can climb out.

Use stones or pebbles to make shallow areas within the pond for birds to stand on.

Include a toad house to provide shelter and shade for your amphibian friends.

Add water-loving plants to your pond to attract all sorts of insects and birds.

⚠ Make sure you never go near a pond without an adult.

Container or bucket · Soil · Stones · Water · Plants

Make a mini pond

Little creatures need a home, birds need water, and people like to observe local wildlife—so let's make everyone happy and build a mini pond! These are perfect additions to your patio, balcony, or yard.

1. Line the container

Use a container or shallow bucket and line it with soil and stones about 2 in (5 cm) deep. This makes a good base.

2. Build an animal exit

Pile some stones up one side of the container so creatures can make their way out if they fall in.

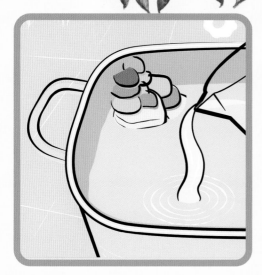

3. Add water

Rainwater is great! Or, if you can, use water from a friend's pond because it is likely to contain pond creatures.

Top tip

Make your pond welcoming to all sorts of creatures by including a mix of features. These could be hiding spots under the water, plants to create shelter, or perches for small birds.

5. Welcome your creatures

Great job! Your mini pond is ready. Now you can watch your little ecosystem grow. Can you spot any creatures?

4. Add plants

Water mint, yellow flag, and iris are all great plants for underwater creatures. Add two or three in the corners.

73

Pond creatures

A pond makes a great habitat for animals that live in or around water. Each of these creatures has a part to play in keeping the pond healthy—and some are food for birds.

Frogs

Frogs live both in and out of the water. They are often found in damp spots, such as under rocks. In the water, they lay frog spawn and eat flies.

Pond snails

These common pond creatures can often be found stuck to the sides of a pond. They are a favorite snack of many birds.

Water hog-lice

These small, shell-covered creatures live at the bottom of ponds. They act as pond cleaners by eating the remains of dead plants.

Observe it!

Do you have your own pond or is there a nearby pond you can visit? Take a trip down to the water with an adult and see which of these creatures you can spot.

Flatworms

Common in ponds, flatworms come in all sizes and colors. They live at the bottom of ponds and are often camouflaged.

More pond animals

Which of these will you be lucky enough to spot?

Great diving beetles

Larvae of great diving beetles are a common pond predator. They eat small worms, tadpoles, and even fish. They dive deep, but always come up for air.

Bat

Pond skater

Mayfly

Caddis fly larvae

These sticky bugs cover their bodies with material from the pond to stay camouflaged. They feed on plants.

Snake

Newts

Newts hide among pond plants and eat flies, larvae, and other small creatures. They lay their spawn in the water.

Toad

CARING FOR BIRDS

Wild animals are very good at taking care of themselves. However, there are things you can do to make sure they are safe in your yard and that they have access to lots of food.

Nesting materials

Every day, there are fewer trees and natural spaces on our planet where birds can nest or find nesting materials. You can help by providing the things birds need.

Twigs

Natural materials

Birds mostly use natural materials to build their nests: things like twigs, leaves, feathers, moss, and hay. If you come across any of these things, you can leave them out for the birds to find.

Leaves

What not to put out

Some materials are not suitable for nests because they can be dangerous for birds if eaten, or if the birds become tangled in them. These include string, mesh, plastic, cellophane, foil, human hair, and plants treated with chemicals.

Top tip

Leave the materials in safe spots that are away from cats and other predators. You could lay them on a feeding tray or hang them from a tree.

Moss

Feathers

DIY ideas

Birds are more likely to find material you put out if it's in a place they might visit anyway. Here are some clever spots.

Block feeder

You can fill a suet-ball feeder with all sorts of materials for birds. These can be accessed safely and easily.

Materials from your home

Some materials you use at home are useful for birds, too, such as cloth strips, yarn, fabric, and shredded paper. Before you throw these items away, think about giving them to your local birds.

Yarn

Wool

Shredded paper

Stocking feeder

Fill the toe end of an old sock or hose with nesting materials. Tie knots to make different sections. Cut holes so the birds can reach the materials.

79

Baby birds

If you're lucky, you may get to watch birds build nests and raise their young. Adult birds work as a team. The female lays the eggs and keeps them warm, while the male brings food and gathers nesting material.

How to spot a baby bird

At breeding time—in the spring and summer—keep an eye out for baby birds. Young birds look different from adults, but not only because they are smaller. Here are a few telltale signs that the bird you've spotted is young.

Gape

The inside of a baby bird's bill is often bright yellow. This is called a gape and the color is a sign of how healthy the bird is.

Young birds show their bright gapes as they open their bills for food.

Inside a nest

If you find a nest near your home, you will hopefully get to see baby birds as they hatch and grow. There are different things to look for at each stage of raising young.

Birds build nests that are secure and safe for laying eggs.

When the adult leaves the nest, it covers the eggs to hide them from predators.

Young starlings have not yet grown their glittering, adult feathers.

Top tip

If you find a baby bird, it's best not to touch it. If it's in a dangerous place, such as near a road, move it very carefully to a close safe spot.

Behavior

Baby birds often act in a funny way when an adult bird comes along with food. They tend to squat down and shake their wings, holding their bills open wide.

An adult Eastern Bluebird places a mealworm into the mouth of its young.

Feathers

Many young birds have duller feathers than adults. The dull color acts as camouflage, helping the young stay hidden from predators.

The eggs are uncovered when the female is ready to start sitting on them.

The female sits on her eggs to keep them warm until they hatch. This takes around a week.

When they first hatch, the young keep their eyes shut, while their feathers start to grow.

When the feathers are fully grown, the young birds are ready to fly short distances.

Keeping watch

There's a lot to learn from watching the comings and goings of birds as they use a nest box. You can help nesting birds—and other birds—by cleaning water sources and ensuring birds are safe from predators.

Nest box guests

It's exciting to watch birds move into a nest box. Looking in the box might disturb them, or even cause the baby birds to fall out. But you can still see and learn a lot while watching from a distance.

This box has a camera inside, with an extra hole that lets in light to film.

- Birds will fly up to an empty box to see if it's the right place for them to nest.

- Once the nest box has been chosen, it is often the female bird's job to carry nesting material to it.

- The female will lay eggs inside and spend time sitting on them to keep them warm. The male may bring her food, or she will leave to find her own.

- Once the chicks are hatched, the female and male will fly to and from the nest box with food.

- After a few weeks, the chicks will leave the nest.

Water care

Depending on the season, there are a few things you can do to keep your birdbath, pond, or dust bath clean and ready to welcome birds.

Fall and winter

Change the water every day or two, so it stays fresh. Wash the birdbath regularly. Float a tennis ball in the birdbath or pond to stop the water from freezing solid.

Spring and summer

Keep the water, soil, or dust filled up and remove any leaves or petals from it. Empty, clean, and refill regularly so it remains safe for birds.

Predator peril

Predators—such as cats—are a danger to birds. Make sure there are no flat surfaces near nest boxes that predators can reach. Birdbaths should offer a good view of the surrounding area so birds can see predators coming.

Think about it!

Look around your outdoor space. Can you see any places where predators can lie in wait for birds?

You will need:

Old wrapping paper   Pencil   Scissors   Glue   Seeds

Seeds for your friends

Growing plants from seeds is a great way to help local wildlife and be kind to birds. Why not invite your friends to join you? Make your own seed packets and pass them out to your friends!

Ask an adult to help!

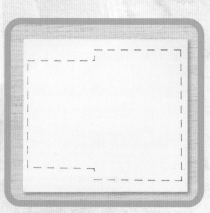

1. Draw the template

On the back of your paper, draw a rough outline of two rectangles connected to each other. One should be bigger than the other.

2. Cut it out

Carefully cut around the outside of your template. It doesn't have to be exact. Don't cut between the two rectangles.

3. Fold in half

Fold your paper along the line where the rectangles meet. The wrapping-paper pattern should be on the outside.

4. Fold the flaps

Fold the edges of the larger rectangle over the smaller rectangle, to create three flaps.

5. Time to glue

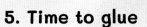

Glue two of the flaps down to create your seed packet. Make sure you glue all the way to the corners.

6. Perfect packet

Pour seeds into your packet and then seal the third flap. Now you're ready to give the packet to one of your friends!

Tell your friends

Let your friends know they can grow their seeds in the ground or in containers. They can even sow them in yogurt cups or egg cartons and grow them on their windowsills. Remember to water the seeds every few days.

Meet an ornithologist!

The author of this book, Dan Rouse, turned her love of birds into a job. She spends most of her time watching birds through her binoculars and talking about them as an expert on the TV and radio. Here is what she has to say about birds.

How did it all begin?
Since the age of three, I have loved birds. My family put up a bird feeder in our yard and so many birds came! I started to notice details about them. I have taken my binoculars and bird-spotting book on every family vacation and day trip since!

Why do you love birds?
I love how you can find birds anywhere and you're never alone when birds are around.

Where do you go to find birds?
Oh, birds can be found anywhere! I live in Wales, and even on a walk to the grocery I might see starlings or a Red Kite. But my favorite place to find birds is on the coast.

How did you become a bird expert?
I wanted to learn more, so I would volunteer: doing bird surveys, working at my local wetland reserve, and going on organized walks. When I was older, I joined a local birding group.

What advice do you have for kids who love birds?
Don't be shy! Talk to people your age and share your love of birds. Just enjoy birds, and get out there and find some!

What is your favorite bird?
The Red-breasted Goose—it is FULL of personality!

Red-breasted Goose

Sparrows

Rüppell's Vulture

What's the coolest thing you've ever seen birds do?
I watched a migration at Spurn Point, an island near Yorkshire, England, I saw thousands of goldfinches, Tree Sparrows, Linnets, and pipits all funnel down the point and off over the sea—it was amazing!

What's your favorite thing about birds?
Every single bird is different. I used to collect Pokémon cards and they all have strengths and weaknesses—and it is the same with birds!

What is the rarest bird you've ever seen?
The rarest bird I've ever seen in the wild is a Rüppell's Vulture—a very large African vulture. I saw it when it was on migration in Portugal.

What can we do to help birds?
We should be trying to protect birds before we lose them. Birds don't care if you live in an apartment or in a house. All you have to do is make the outdoor spaces near you a little more welcoming for birds.

What is your best birdwatching tip?
Enjoy it! Birding is supposed to be fun.

> **"Birds share our world. For me, they have been and always will be a vital part of my life."**

Bird profiles

Use these profiles to help identify some of
the birds you might see near your home.

Sharp-shinned Hawk

This bird of prey hunts smaller birds and
uses its sharp bill to tear up its food.

Length 10—14 in (25—34 cm)
Wingspan 21—26 in (53—65 cm) **Call** Mainly
silent, with a high "kewkewkew" alarm call

Great Horned Owl

These owls often use the old nests of other big
birds, such as crows or hawks.

Length 1½ ft (0.5 m) **Wingspan** 3½ ft (1.1 m)

Call Deep hoots of "hoohooh hoo hoo"

Blue Jay

Both the males and females have bright blue
and white colors on their tails and wings.

Length 9½—12 in (24—30 cm) **Wingspan** 16 in
(41 cm) **Call** Harsh scream of "Jay! Jay!"

American Crow

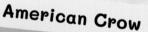

This all-black bird will eat almost anything.
It is very intelligent and curious.

Length 16—20 in (40—50 cm) **Wingspan** 35—40 in
(89—102 cm) **Call** Loud "caaw-caaw-caaw"

Mourning Dove

These doves can be identified by black spots on their faces and wings.

Length 9–13½ in (23–34 cm)   **Wingspan** 18 in (46 cm)   **Call** Mournful (sad) cooing

Downy Woodpecker

Red spot on male

The drum of a bill on a tree could be caused by this or another woodpecker looking for insects.

Length 7 in (17 cm)   **Wingspan** 12 in (30 cm)   **Call** "chr, chr, chrchrchr"

Baltimore Oriole

In addition to insects, this bird loves fruit and will visit feeders to feast on sliced oranges.

Length 8–10 in (20–26 cm)   **Wingspan** 10–12 in (26–30 cm)   **Call** Flutelike one or two notes

Ruby-throated Hummingbird

Found in the Eastern US, this bird dips its long, thin bill into flowers to drink nectar.

Length 3–3½ in (7–9 cm)   **Wingspan** 3–4½ in (8–11 cm)   **Call** Buzzy call to drive off threats

Cedar Waxwing

This acrobatic bird uses its long claws to cling to branches as it hangs upside down to feed on berries.

Length 6—7 in (15—18 cm) **Wingspan** 9—12 in (23—30 cm) **Call** Whistle of "tre-e-e-e-e"

Yellow Warbler

Short bill for picking up insects from leaves.

The yellow feathers of this bird are brighter on the male than on the female.

Length 4½—5 in (11—13 cm) **Wingspan** 6—9 in (16—22 cm) **Call** Breeding call said to sound like "sweet-sweet-I'm-so-sweet"

Barn Swallow

The triangular, wide-gaped bill of this bird allows it to capture insects in flight.

Length 6.5—7½ in (17—19 cm) **Wingspan** 12½—13½ in (32—34.5 cm) **Call** Cheerful warble and clacking sound

Purple Martin

Male Purple Martins are blueish black all over.

The female looks different than the male, with a gray-brown forehead, throat, and belly.

Length 7—8 in (18—20 cm) **Wingspan** 15—16 in (38—41 cm) **Call** Croaks, chortles, and rattles

Warbling Vireo

This bird can often be seen hopping along high-up tree branches, looking for insects.

Length 5 in (12-13 cm) **Wingspan** 8½ in (22 cm)
Call Wide variety of songs, which may sound similar to the robin

Red breast

American Robin

The stout, orange-yellow bill of this bird is often plunged into the ground to find worms.

Length 8—11 in (20—28 cm) **Wingspan** 12—16 in (30—41 cm) **Call** Repeated, rising and falling song

Eastern Bluebird

In the US, this bird is only found in the Eastern states—but the Western Bluebird found in the Western states is almost identical!

Length 6—8 in (15—20 cm) **Wingspan** 10—13 in (25—33 cm) **Call** Musical "churr-wi"

Only the males are a bright red color.

Northern Cardinal

This bird can be spotted in the Eastern US, usually eating insects on the ground in summer and seeds and berries in the winter.

Length 8—9 in (21—23 cm) **Wingspan** 10—12 in (25—30cm) **Call** "Tik" or "cheer-cheercheer"

**Black crown
on top of head**

Black-capped Chickadee

The small, sharp bill of this bird is used to crack open seeds.

Length 4—6 in (10—15 cm) **Wingspan** 6—8 in (15—20 cm) **Call** Song whistle of "fee-bee" and alarm call of "chick-a-dee-dee-dee"

White-breasted Nuthatch

Nuthatches creep along tree trunks and branches, using their bills to pluck insects and seeds from cracks in the bark.

Length 5—5½ in (13—14 cm) **Wingspan** 8—11 in (20—27 cm) **Call** Different calls and songs

Northern Mockingbird

From its high perch, this bird can be heard repeating the stolen songs of other birds.

Length 8½—10 in (22—25 cm) **Wingspan** 13—15 in (33—38 cm) **Call** Mimics other calls

Chipping Sparrow

Males and females have similar markings, which include white eyebrows.

Length 5—6 in (13—15 cm) **Wingspan** 8—9 in (20—23 cm) **Call** Hard "tsip" while foraging

European Starling

Starlings often fly in huge flocks, all swooping and diving together in what looks like a dance.

Length 8 in (20 cm) **Wingspan** 16 in (40 cm)
Call Loud whistles, "schreeer" sounds, and a buzzy "zzeeri-zzeeri-zzeeri"

Male House Sparrows have black chins.

House Sparrow

These birds can miss out on food if other, more aggressive birds are around. They benefit from a second feeder hung nearby.

Length 6 in (15 cm) **Wingspan** 9 in (23 cm)
Call Loud "chirrups" and "cheeps"

American Goldfinch

The male goldfinch has a lemon-yellow body. This bird's long, triangular bill is the perfect shape for digging into seed heads.

Length 4–5 in (10–14 cm) **Wingspan** 7½–9 in (19–23 cm) **Call** "Per-twee-twee-twee" in flight

House Wren

Wrens don't feed from garden feeders—they prefer to eat bugs, including spiders!

Length 4½–5 in (11–13 cm) **Wingspan** 6–7 in (15–16.5 cm) **Call** Energetic stuttering, bubbly series of sounds

Glossary

Amphibian Creature that can live both in and out of water

Aphid Type of very small insect

Bird of prey Bird that hunts and eats other animals

Breed Produce babies

Camouflage Blend in with the surroundings

Climate Average weather in an area

Compost Natural materials that have decayed. When added to soil, it helps plants grow better

Deciduous Tree that loses its leaves in the fall

Decline Go down

Eaves Where the roof hangs over the walls of a building

Ecosystem Group of animals and plants that live and interact with each other in one area

Foliage Leaves of plants

Foraging Searching for food

Gape Bright yellow mouth of a baby bird

Habitat Where an animal or plant has everything it needs to live

Harvest Gather seeds or crops

Larvae Young insects that have hatched from eggs but haven't yet turned into their adult form

Mammal Warm-blooded animal that gives birth to live young

Migrate Move to a different country or climate as the seasons change

Nectar Sweet liquid produced in flowers that attracts insects

Nutrients Chemicals in food that help animals and plants grow and thrive

Organic Completely natural—with no added chemicals

Ornithologist Bird expert

Pellet Small ball or piece of something

Predator Animal that hunts another animal

Roost Settle down for a rest

Shrub Plant that is like a tree but smaller, with leaves close to the ground

Species Group of the same animals or plants

Suet Animal fat, usually from beef

Territorial Protective of their space

Index

DK | Penguin Random House

UK Editorial Shari Last, Kathleen Teece
US Senior Editor Shannon Beatty
US Editor Margaret Parrish
Design Kanika Kalra, Sonny Flynn
Additional Design Bharti Karakoti, Bhagyashree Nayak, Mohd. Zishan, Roohi Rais
Jacket Designer Sonny Flynn
Project Picture Researcher Rituraj Singh
Production Editor Dragana Puvacic
Production controllers Magdalena Bojko, Leanne Burke
DTP designers Sachin Gupta, Vikram Singh, Vijay Kandwal
Managing Editor Jonathan Melmoth
Managing Art Editors Diane Peyton Jones, Ivy Sengupta
Publishing Coordinator Issy Walsh
Delhi Creative Heads Glenda Fernandes, Malavika Talukder
Deputy art Director Mabel Chan
Publishing Director Sarah Larter

Illustrations by Abby Cook
Consultant Joseph DiCostanzo

First American Edition, 2023
Published in the United States by DK Publishing
1745 Broadway, 20th Floor, New York, NY 10019

Copyright © 2023 Dorling Kindersley Limited
A Penguin Random House Company
23 24 25 26 27 10 9 8 7 6 5 4 3
005–333761–Jan/2023

All rights reserved.
Without limiting the rights under the copyright reserved above, no part of this publication may be reproduced, stored in or introduced into a retrieval system, or transmitted, in any form, or by any means (electronic, mechanical, photocopying, recording, or otherwise), without the prior written permission of the copyright owner.
Published in Great Britain by Dorling Kindersley Limited

A catalog record for this book is available from the Library of Congress.
ISBN: 978-0-7440-7280-8

DK books are available at special discounts when purchased in bulk for sales promotions, premiums, fund-raising, or educational use. For details, contact: DK Publishing Special Markets, 1745 Broadway, 20th Floor, New York, NY 10019
SpecialSales@dk.com

Printed and bound in China

For the curious
www.dk.com

MIX
Paper | Supporting responsible forestry
FSC www.fsc.org FSC™ C018179

This book was made with Forest Stewardship Council™ certified paper - one small step in DK's commitment to a sustainable future.
For more information go to www.dk.com/our-green-pledge

Acknowledgments

Dorling Kindersley would like to thank Marie Greenwood for editorial assistance, Polly Goodman for proofreading, and Helen Peters for the index.

Discover more birds and nature at www.danrouse.org.uk/kidscorner

Picture credits

The publisher would like to thank the following for their kind permission to reproduce their photographs: (Key: a-above; b-below/bottom; c-centre; f-far; l-left; r-right; t-top)

1 Alamy Stock Photo: Ivan Kuzmin (clb). Dreamstime.com: Steve Byland (cra). **2** Dreamstime.com: Brian Lasenby (cl); Mikelane45 (ca); Leerobin (x2/cb). **3** Dreamstime.com: Moose Henderson (tc); Scphoto48 (tc/feeder). **4** Alamy Stock Photo: Richard Higgins (cra). **5** Alamy Stock Photo: DanitaDelimont.com / Richard & Susan Day (crb); Karen Patterson (tr). Getty Images / iStock: Janet Griffin-Scott (tl). **6** Dorling Kindersley: Robert Royse (clb). Dreamstime.com: Charles Brutlag (cl); Jillian Cain (bc). Getty Images / iStock: MattCuda (br). **7** Alamy Stock Photo: Richard Buchbinder (tr). Dreamstime.com: Assanta (bc). **8** Alamy Stock Photo: Gaertner (b). **9** Dreamstime.com: Steve Byland (br); Petar Kremenarov (cla); Megan Lorenz (bc). **10** Alamy Stock Photo: Johann Schumacher (cr). Dreamstime.com: Petar Kremenarov (crb). **11** Dreamstime.com: Michael Truchon / Mtruchon (crb); Michael Truchon (tr). **12** Alamy Stock Photo: David Nelson (clb). Getty Images: Gary Carter / Corbis Documentary (cr). **13** Alamy Stock Photo: Ivan Kuzmin (crb). Dreamstime.com: Charles Brutlag (cla). **14** Dreamstime.com: John Anderson (crb). Getty Images: Diana Robinson Photography / Moment (cla). **15** Dreamstime.com: Glenn Price (clb). **16** Alamy Stock Photo: blickwinkel / M. Woike (cb); Klaus Steinkamp (tr); Larry Ditto / Danita Delimont (cl). Depositphotos Inc: bsd (bl/Sun, tr/Sun). Dreamstime.com: Hakan Ertan (x2/t); Golden Sikorka (x3). **17** Alamy Stock Photo: Ben3images (cb); Jussi Murtosaari / Nature Picture Library (cl). Dreamstime.com: Hakan Ertan (x2); Golden Sikorka (x3); Olga Novoseletska (x2/br). Getty Images / iStock: ulimi / DigitalVision Vectors (x6). Shutterstock.com: Jukka Jantunen (ca). **18** Alamy Stock Photo: Laura Romin & Larry Dalton (cr). Dorling Kindersley: Natural History Museum, London (bc); Natural History Museum, London (br). Dreamstime.com: Steve Byland (clb); K Quinn Ferris (tr); Wildphotos (crb). **19** Alamy Stock Photo: Chris Gomersall (tc); Richard Higgins (cr). Dorling Kindersley: Natural History Museum, London (bl); Natural History Museum, London (br). Dreamstime.com: Michael Truchon / Mtruchon (cb). Getty Images / iStock: drakuliren (cla). **20** Dreamstime.com: Gerald Deboer (cr); K Quinn Ferris (cl). **21** Alamy Stock Photo: Bill Draker / Rolf Nussbaumer Photography (cla). Dreamstime.com: Rinus Baak (cr). **22-23** Alamy Stock Photo: Richard Buchbinder. **23** Getty Images / iStock: Janet Griffin-Scott (cl). **24** Dreamstime.com: Paul Roedding (cl); Wei Kee Teoh (crb). **25** Alamy Stock Photo: Sharon Talson (cra). Dreamstime.com: Forestpath (clb). **26-27** Dreamstime.com: Tashka2000. **26** Alamy Stock Photo: Janet Horton (bc); Cindy Sutton (cl). Dreamstime.com: Bert Folsom (clb); Freeskyline (cra). **27** Alamy Stock Photo: B LaRue (bl); Linda McKusick (tl). Dreamstime.com: Oksana Ermak (clb, bc); Heathse (c); Andrey Starostin (tc); Irina Onufrieva (br). **28** Dreamstime.com: Amphaiwan (cla/Bowl); Josep Curto (x2/t); Jgade (cla); Isabel Poulin (ca); BrightonGranny (cra). Shutterstock.com: Sarah2 (br). 28-29 Dreamstime.com: Tashka2000. **29** Dreamstime.com: Chernetskaya (cr); Erika Pichoud (br). **30** Alamy Stock Photo: Daybreak Imagery (tr); John Van Decker (bl). naturepl.com: David Tipling (crb). **31** Dreamstime.com: Moose Henderson (tr); Brian Kushner (cla); Steveheap (crb). wildlifeworld.co.uk. **32** Alamy Stock Photo: Philip Mugridge (cra). Dreamstime.com: Birdiegal717 (crb). Getty Images / iStock: BrianLasenby (cl). **33** Alamy Stock Photo: Michael Cummings (tl); Tom Ingram (clb). Shutterstock.com: Simon J Beer (cra); mizy (br). **34** Shutterstock.com: Mariyana M (cla/Bottle); shpakdm (cla); MNI (ca/Scissor); photka (ca); xpixel (cra). **35** Dreamstime.com: Denis Dore (crb); Gerald Marella (cra). **36-37** Alamy Stock Photo: blickwinkel. **38** Alamy Stock Photo: Oleh Honcharenko (cr). Dreamstime.com: Jessamine (br); NatmacStock (crb); David Jones (cra). **39** Dreamstime.com: Melvin Ray Herr (cl); Bruce Macqueen (tr); Thejipen (cra). **40** Alamy Stock Photo: Sheree Sedgbeer (cr). CJ Wildlife: www.birdfood.co.uk: (bl). Dreamstime.com: Melinda Fawver (crb); Valiva (l). **40-41** Dreamstime.com: Bugtiger. **41** Dreamstime.com: Melinda Fawver (tl); Mike Trewet (bl); Kazakovmaksim (tr); Valiva (r). wildlifeworld.co.uk. **42** Alamy Stock Photo: Paul Mogford (bl). Dreamstime.com: Jillian Cain (cr); Valiva (l); Melinda Fawver (cra). wildlifeworld.co.uk. **42-43** Dreamstime.com: Bugtiger; Melinda Fawver (t). **43** Dreamstime.com: Akinshin (bc); Valiva (r); Melinda Fawver (clb, x2/br); Ksushsh (tr). Shutterstock.com: Miroslav Milda (cla, crb). wildlifeworld.co.uk. **44** naturepl.com: Alan Murphy / BIA (tr). wildlifeworld.co.uk. **45** Dreamstime.com: Irina Onufrieva (br). **46** Alamy Stock Photo: Paul Mogford (tr). Dreamstime.com: Charles Brutlag (bl/titmouse); Petar Kremenarov (bl). wildlifeworld.co.uk. **47** CJ Wildlife: www.birdfood.co.uk: (tc). **48-49** Alamy Stock Photo: Doris Dumrauf. **50** Shutterstock.com: Miroslav Milda (clb). **51** Dorling Kindersley: Robert Royse (clb). Dreamstime.com: Steve Byland (tr). **52** Dorling Kindersley: Downderry Nursery (ca); RHS Wisley (cra); Neil Fletcher (cb); RHS Wisley (crb); RHS Wisley (crb/daphne laureola). **53** Alamy Stock Photo: Bob Gibbons (tr). Dorling Kindersley: RHS Wisley (tc); RHS Wisley (cb). **54** 123RF.com: Leonid Ikan (c); timyee (cl). Dreamstime.com: Yuliya Borodina (tc). **55** Depositphotos Inc: swimwitdafishes (cb). Dreamstime.com: Jeans550 (cla); Calvin L. Leake (tc); Poravute Siriphiroon (c). **56** Dreamstime.com: Natalia Bachkova (c); Leerobin (cl); Sushil Chikane (clb). **57** Alamy Stock Photo: blickwinkel / McPHOTO / H.-R. Mueller (tl); Alistair Scott (tc). Dreamstime.com: Natalia Bachkova (crb); Radub85 (tr); Marekusz (cl); Tamara Kulikova (br). **58** Dorling Kindersley: Stephen Oliver (clb). Dreamstime.com: Anton Starikov (cla). Getty Images / iStock: stocknshares (crb). **58-59** 123RF.com: Saichol Modepradit. **59** Alamy Stock Photo: John Van Decker (clb); FLPA (tl). **60** Dreamstime.com: Elisabeth Burrell (tc/water); Roman Ivaschenko (tl); Tamara Kulikova (tc); Photka (tr); Isselee (tr/tit, cla). **61** Dreamstime.com: Vasyl Helevachuk (cr). **62-63** Alamy Stock Photo: DanitaDelimont / Rolf Nussbaumer. **64** Dreamstime.com: Mikelane45 (c). **65** Alamy Stock Photo: Art Phaneuf (tl). Dreamstime.com: Charles Brutlag (crb). **66** Shutterstock.com: Danita Delimont (cl). **67** Alamy Stock Photo: BC Photo (clb); Claudine Weber-Hilty (tr). **68** Alamy Stock Photo: blickwinkel / F. Hecker (x2/cb). Dreamstime.com: Ratana21 (tl); Snowwhiteimages (tc). **69** Alamy Stock Photo: blickwinkel / F. Hecker (clb). Dorling Kindersley: Stephen Oliver (br). Dreamstime.com: Lnsdes (clb/granite); Valentina Razumova (clb/rocks). **70** Alamy Stock Photo: Ellen McKnight (cb/bullfrog). Dreamstime.com: Andrey Prokuronov (cb); Rck953 (ca). **71** Alamy Stock Photo: Arterra Picture Library / Arndt Sven-Erik (cra); Toby Houlton (ca). Dorling Kindersley: Forrest L. Mitchell / James Laswel (cl). Dreamstime.com: Natalya Aksenova (clb); Serhii Suravikin (crb); Andrii Medvediuk (bc). wildlifeworld.co.uk: (c). **72** Dreamstime.com: Alexandr Labetskiy (tc/stones); Wabeno (tl); Rimglow (tc); Pavel Lipskiy (tr/water); Elena Zlatomrezova (tr). **73** Dreamstime.com: Assanta (bc). **74** Alamy Stock Photo: Skip Moody / Dembinsky Photo Associates (cra); Papilio / Robert Pickett (cl); DP Wildlife Invertebrates (bc). **75** Alamy Stock Photo: blickwinkel / A. Hartl (bl); Lee Rentz (cr); ClassicStock / J. PATTON (cra); Kevin Szen (cr/Mayfly, br). Dreamstime.com: Denboma (cla); Valentina Moraru (crb). Getty Images: Thomas Kline / Design Pics (tc, cb). **76-77** Alamy Stock Photo: Ivan Kuzmin. **78** 123RF.com: picsfive (cra/note). Alamy Stock Photo: Robert Clay (clb). Dreamstime.com: Dianazh (pebbles); Piolka (cra); Melinda Fawver (cr); Ksushsh (tr). **78-79** Dreamstime.com: Kriangkraiwut Boonlom; Logomimi (tc). **79** 123RF.com: picsfive (clb). Dreamstime.com: Piolka (cla). **80** Alamy Stock Photo: George E Stewart / Dembinsky Photo Associates (c). Dreamstime.com: Agami Photo Agency (tr). **81** Alamy Stock Photo: Toby Houlton (cla); Karen Patterson (crb). Dreamstime.com: Natalia Bachkova (cr). **82** Alamy Stock Photo: Liam Bunce (clb). Dreamstime.com: Charles Brutlag (tc). **83** Alamy Stock Photo: David Bratley (bc). Dorling Kindersley: Robert Royse (clb). **84-85** Dreamstime.com: Chutyching (texturex6). **84** Dorling Kindersley: Kanika Kalra (clb, cb, crb). Dreamstime.com: Irashi (tc/Glue); Andrey Starostin (tr); Irina Kryvasheina (cla). Shutterstock.com: LightField Studios (bc); MNI (tc, cb/scissors). **85** Dorling Kindersley: Kanika Kalra (tl, tc, clb); Dave King / Rotring UK Ltd (cra). Dreamstime.com: Irashi (ca); Mirage3 (cr). Shutterstock.com: FotoHelin (br). **86** Dreamstime.com: Elena Podolnaya (br). **88** Alamy Stock Photo: Nature Picture Library (cra). Dreamstime.com: K Quinn Ferris (clb); Petar Kremenarov (cla); Slowmotiongli (crb). **89** Dorling Kindersley: Tom Grey (cla). Dreamstime.com: Steve Byland (cra); Linnette Engler (clb). Getty Images / iStock: MattCuda (br). **90** Dorling Kindersley: Alan Murphy (cra). Dreamstime.com: Dennis Donohue (cla); Mikelane45 (clb); Imogen Warren (br). **91** Alamy Stock Photo: All Canada Photos / Nick Saunders (cla). Dreamstime.com: Steve Byland (clb); Petar Kremenarov (cra); Stevenrussellsmithphotos (crb). **92** Dreamstime.com: Rinus Baak (clb); Brian Lasenby (cla); Gerald Marella (cra); Sue Feldberg (crb). **93** Dreamstime.com: Steve Byland (crb); Petr Simon (cla); Dalia Kvedaraite (cra); Wildphotos (clb). **94** Dreamstime.com: Assanta (bc). Getty Images / iStock: drakuliren (tc). **95** Getty Images / iStock: Janet Griffin-Scott (tr) **Cover images:** Front: Alamy Stock Photo: AGAMI Photo Agency / Chris van Rijswijk bl, Minden Pictures / Steve Gettle tr; Dorling Kindersley: Alan Murphy clb; Dreamstime.com: Charles Brutlag tc, Steve Byland br, Svetlana Foote ca, Petar Kremenarov crb, Llmckinne bc, Michael Truchon cb, Imogen Warren tl; Back: Dreamstime.com: Mark Hryciw clb, Jgorzynik tc, Mikelane45 tl, Vasiliy Vishnevskiy crb; naturepl.com: Alan Murphy / BIA tr; Spine: naturepl.com: Alan Murphy / BIA All other images © Dorling Kindersley